● i DISCOVER
MY FIRST LIBRARY OF KNOWLEDGE

PLANET
EARTH

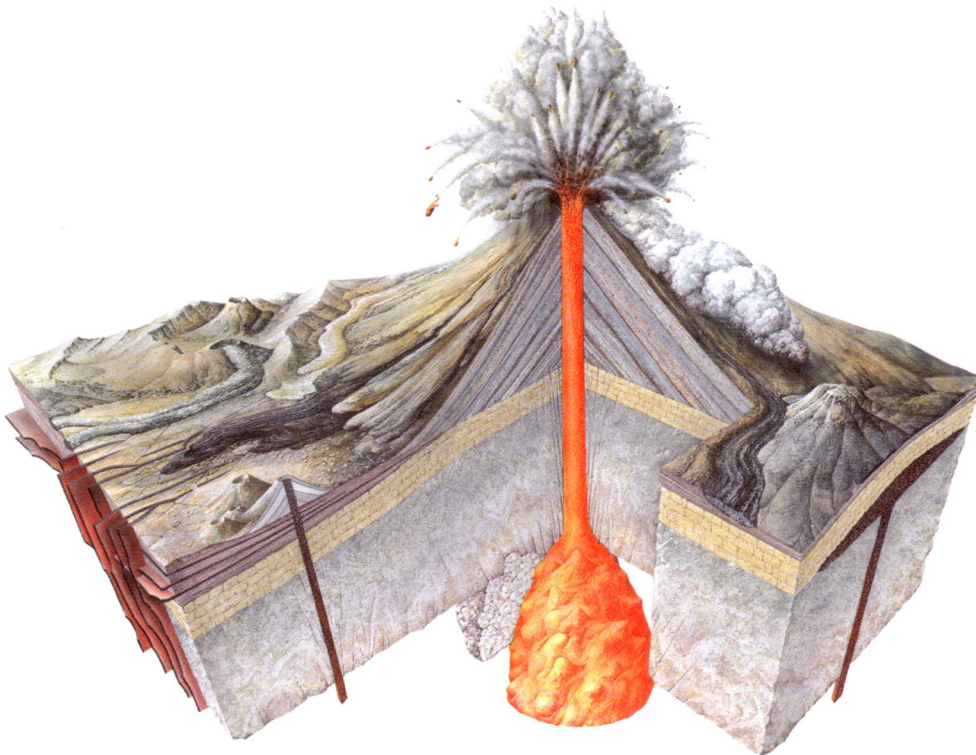

HB
HINKLER BOOKS

HINKLER BOOKS

I Discover My First Library of Knowledge: Planet Earth

This edition first published in 2006 by Hinkler Books Pty Ltd
45–55 Fairchild Street Heatherton Victoria 3202 Australia
www.hinklerbooks.com

Copyright ©2005 Orpheus Books Ltd.

10 9 8 7 6 5 4
10 09 08

Original edition first published in English under the title of
My First Library of Knowledge, in 2005 by Orpheus Books Ltd.,
6 Church Green, Witney, Oxfordshire, OX28 4AW

Cover design: Peter Tovey Studio

Created and produced by Rachel Coombs, Nicholas Harris,
Sarah Harrison, Sarah Hartley and Emma Helbrough, Orpheus Books Ltd.

Text: Nicholas Harris

Consultant: Susanna van Rose

Illustrated by Gary Hincks and Peter Dennis

Prepress: Graphic Print Group

Cased edition ISBN: 1 7415 7572 9
Paperback edition ISBN: 1 7415 7598 2
Printed and bound in China

CONTENTS

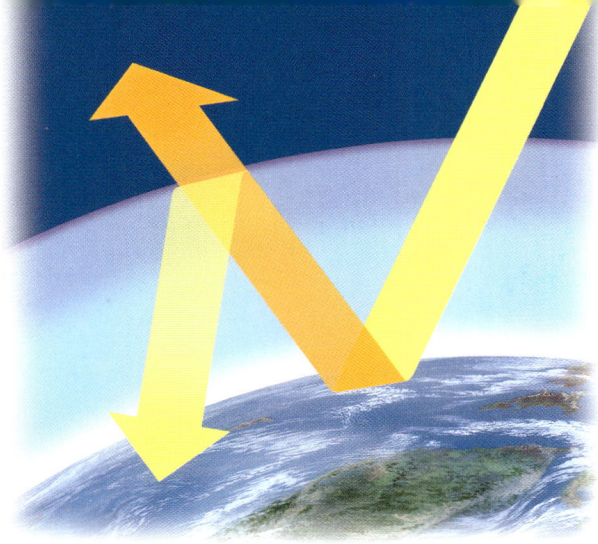

INTRODUCTION

THE EARTH is a huge, spinning ball of rock. It is one of nine planets that travel around the Sun. It is the only world we know where life exists. Its surface is made up of oceans, which cover more than two thirds of it, and land masses, called continents. A layer of air called the atmosphere surrounds the Earth.

INSIDE THE EARTH

THE EARTH has a thin rocky shell on the outside, called the crust. Beneath lie several layers, all extremely hot. The first layer, the mantle, is made of rocks so hot they have partly melted. Farther down is the outer core, made of liquid metal. The inner core, at the Earth's centre, is a solid ball of iron.

MAGMA

In the mantle, the temperature is 2000°C. Here, the rock is partly melted. Known as magma, it flows like hot tarmac on a newly-surfaced road. Sometimes the magma is forced upwards from the mantle. It can burst through weak points in the Earth's crust. It erupts at the surface in a volcano.

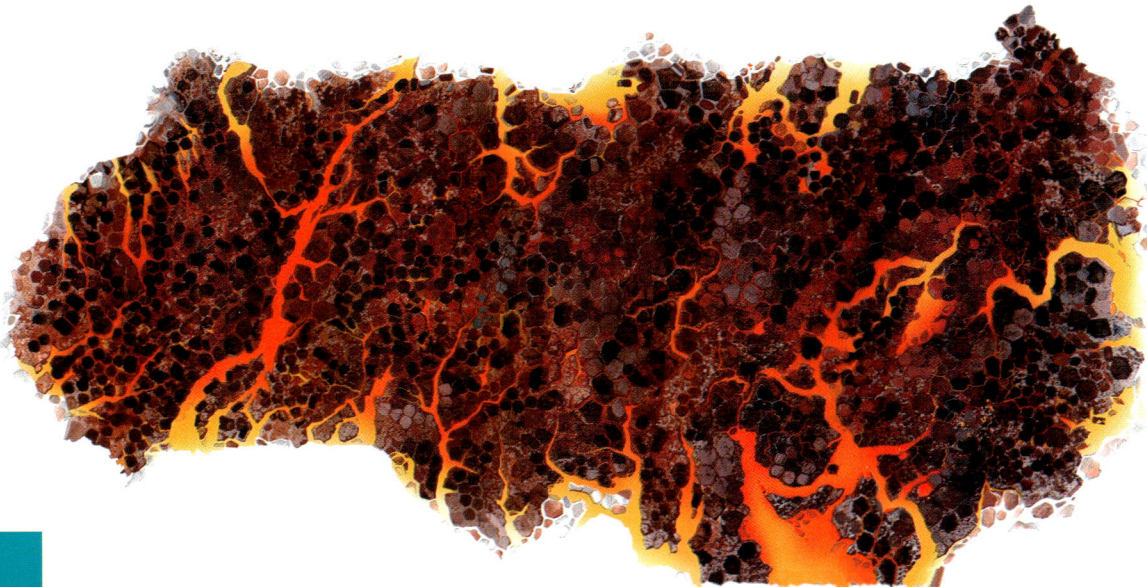

In this illustration, a large slice of the Earth has been cut away so we can see the layers inside.

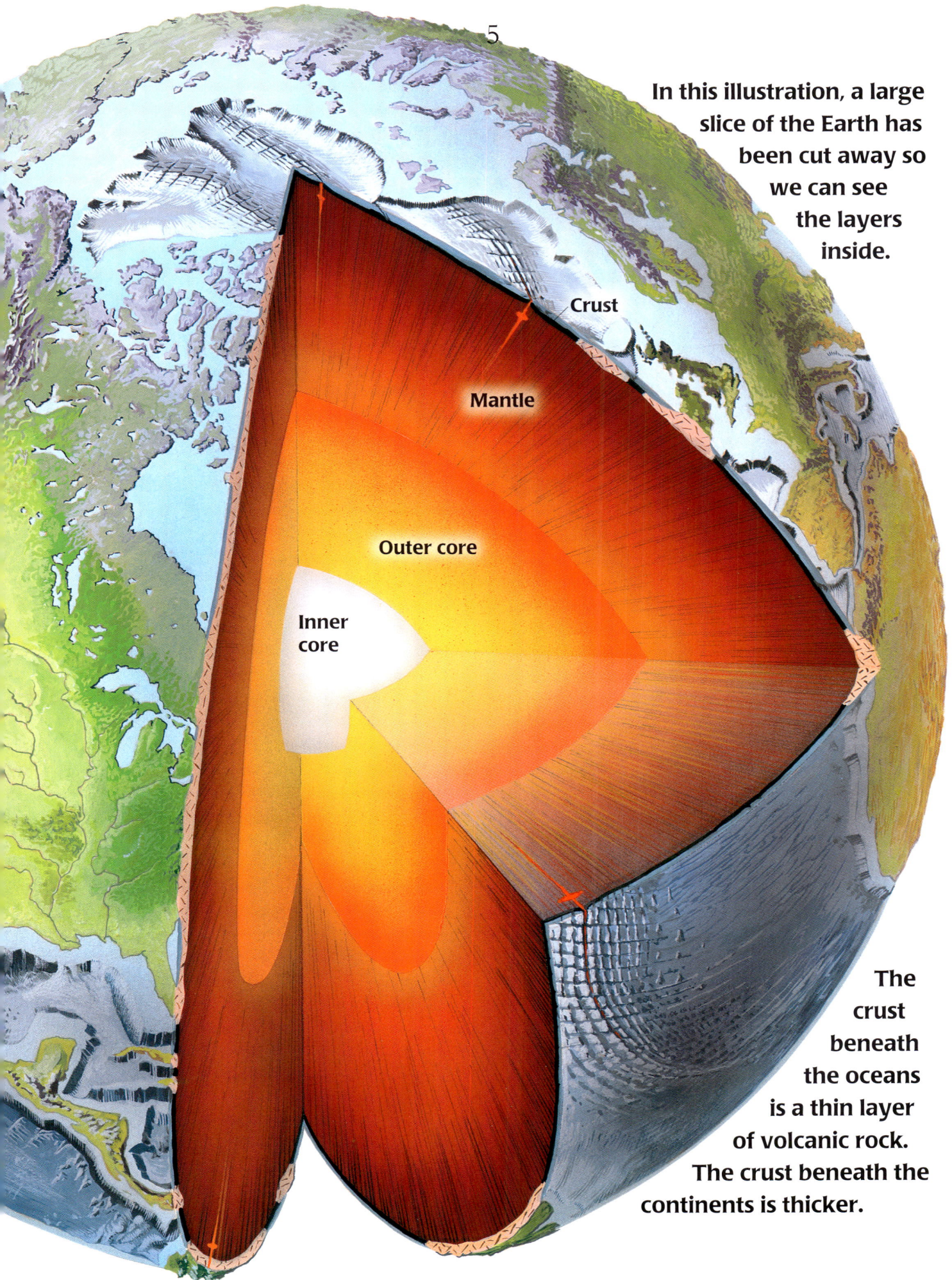

Crust

Mantle

Outer core

Inner core

The crust beneath the oceans is a thin layer of volcanic rock. The crust beneath the continents is thicker.

TECTONIC PLATES

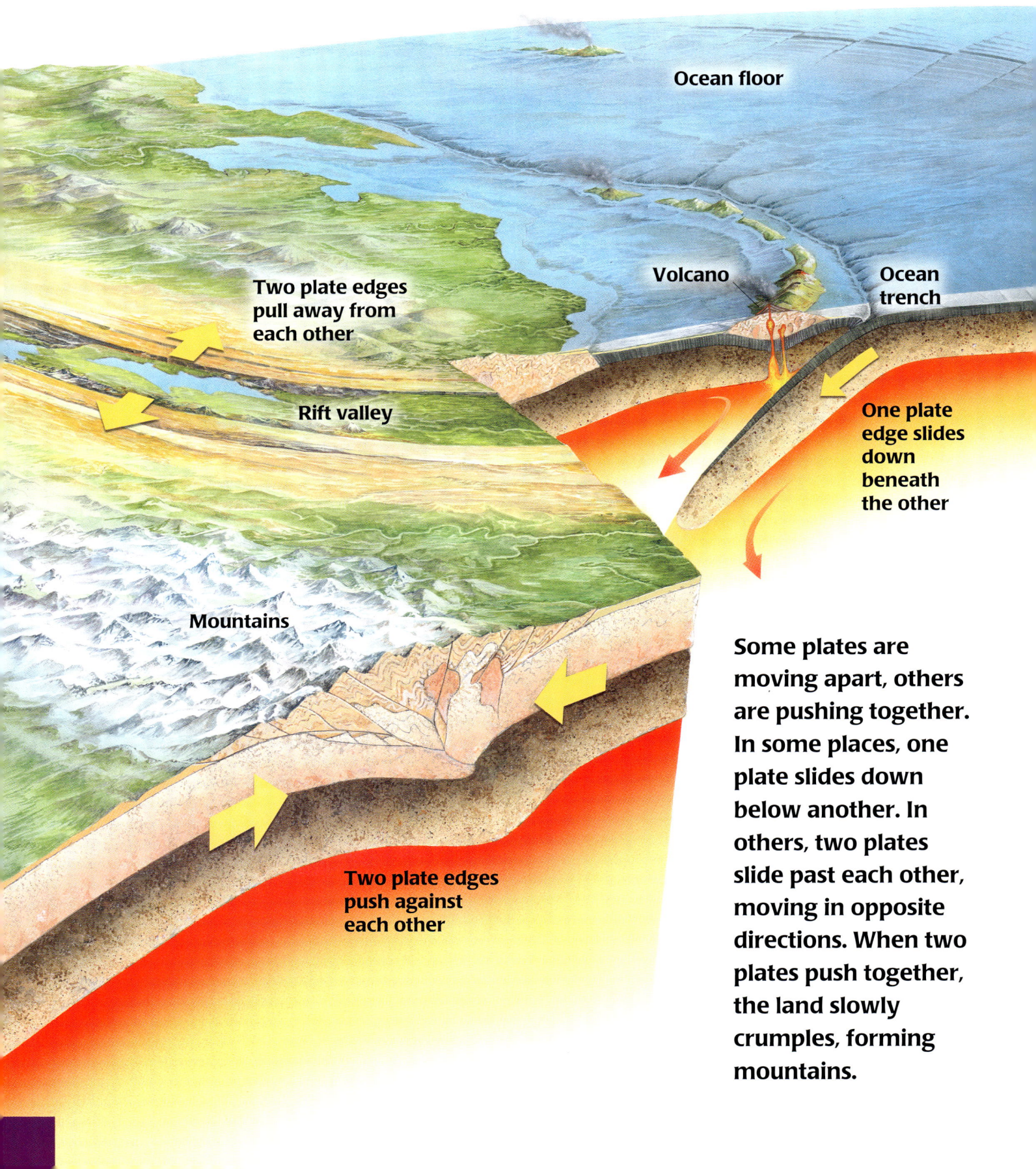

Ocean floor

Volcano

Ocean trench

Two plate edges pull away from each other

Rift valley

One plate edge slides down beneath the other

Mountains

Two plate edges push against each other

Some plates are moving apart, others are pushing together. In some places, one plate slides down below another. In others, two plates slide past each other, moving in opposite directions. When two plates push together, the land slowly crumples, forming mountains.

This diagram is a cross-section through the Earth's crust. The yellow arrows show which way the plates are moving.

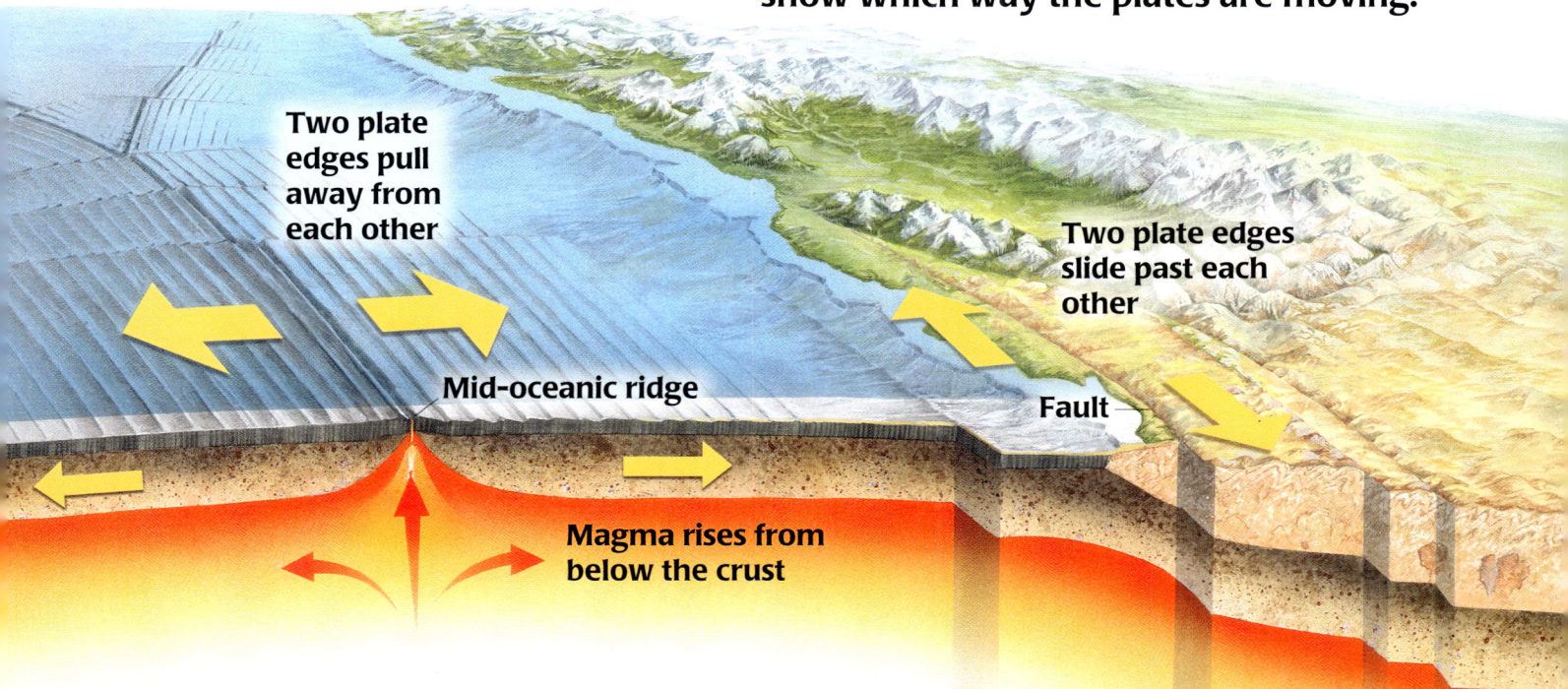

Two plate edges pull away from each other

Two plate edges slide past each other

Mid-oceanic ridge

Fault

Magma rises from below the crust

THE EARTH's surface is like a jigsaw puzzle wrapped around a giant ball. It is divided into about 15 jagged-edge pieces, called tectonic plates. They are always shifting about, but only gradually. Sometimes they lock together for a time, then suddenly jolt apart, causing earthquakes.

The white lines on this globe mark some of the tectonic plate edges. One runs like an enormous crack down the middle of the Atlantic Ocean.

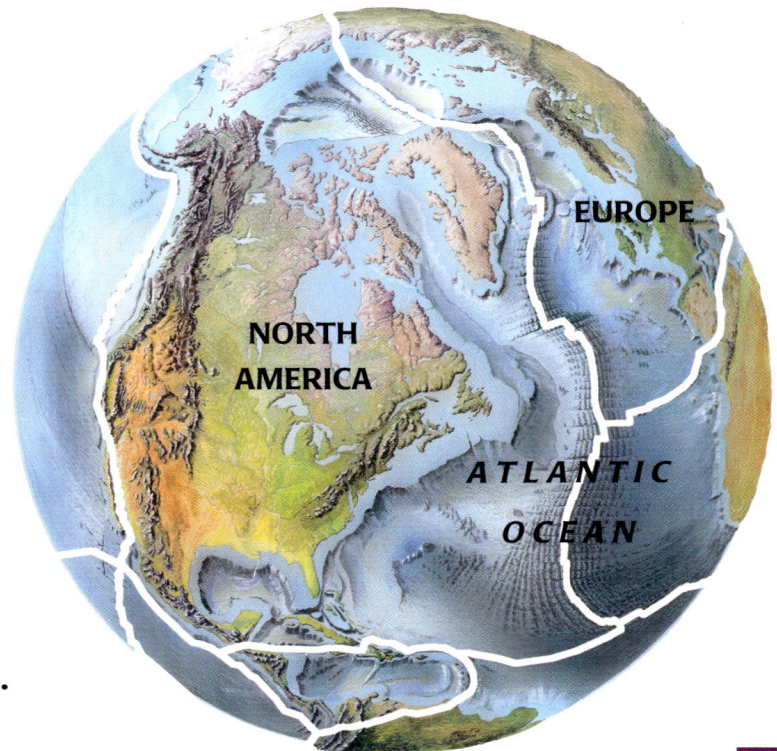

EUROPE

NORTH AMERICA

ATLANTIC OCEAN

VOLCANOES

A VOLCANO is an opening in the Earth's crust through which magma erupts. Many volcanoes are cone-shaped mountains with a crater at the summit.

In a violent eruption, the volcano shoots huge amounts of lava (erupted magma), ash and dust into the air. Over time, many layers of lava and ash and dust build up.

Lava bombs

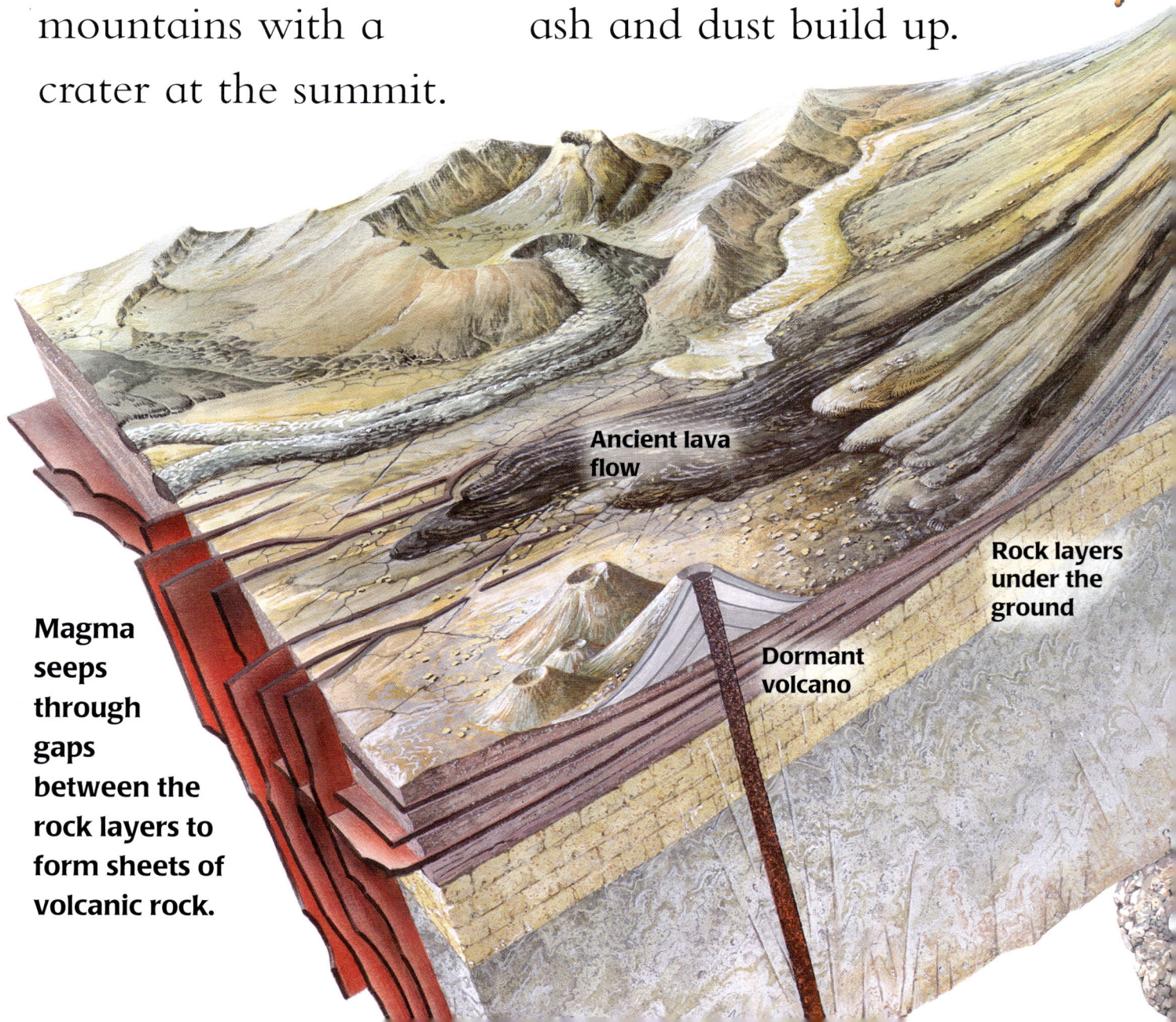

Ancient lava flow

Rock layers under the ground

Dormant volcano

Magma seeps through gaps between the rock layers to form sheets of volcanic rock.

Ash cloud

Crater

Cloud of ash, dust and glowing gas

Layers of lava and ash from previous eruptions

Vent

Magma

Ancient lava flow

Extinct volcano

Cooled magma

TYPES OF VOLCANO

An active volcano erupts lava, ash and dust frequently. When a volcano has not erupted for many years, it is called a dormant volcano. But this type of volcano may erupt again some time in the future. When eruptions stop altogether, the volcano is described as extinct. Some volcanoes blast out red-hot lava and gas in spectacular explosions. But in many other volcanoes, the lava oozes out gently, like boiling syrup.

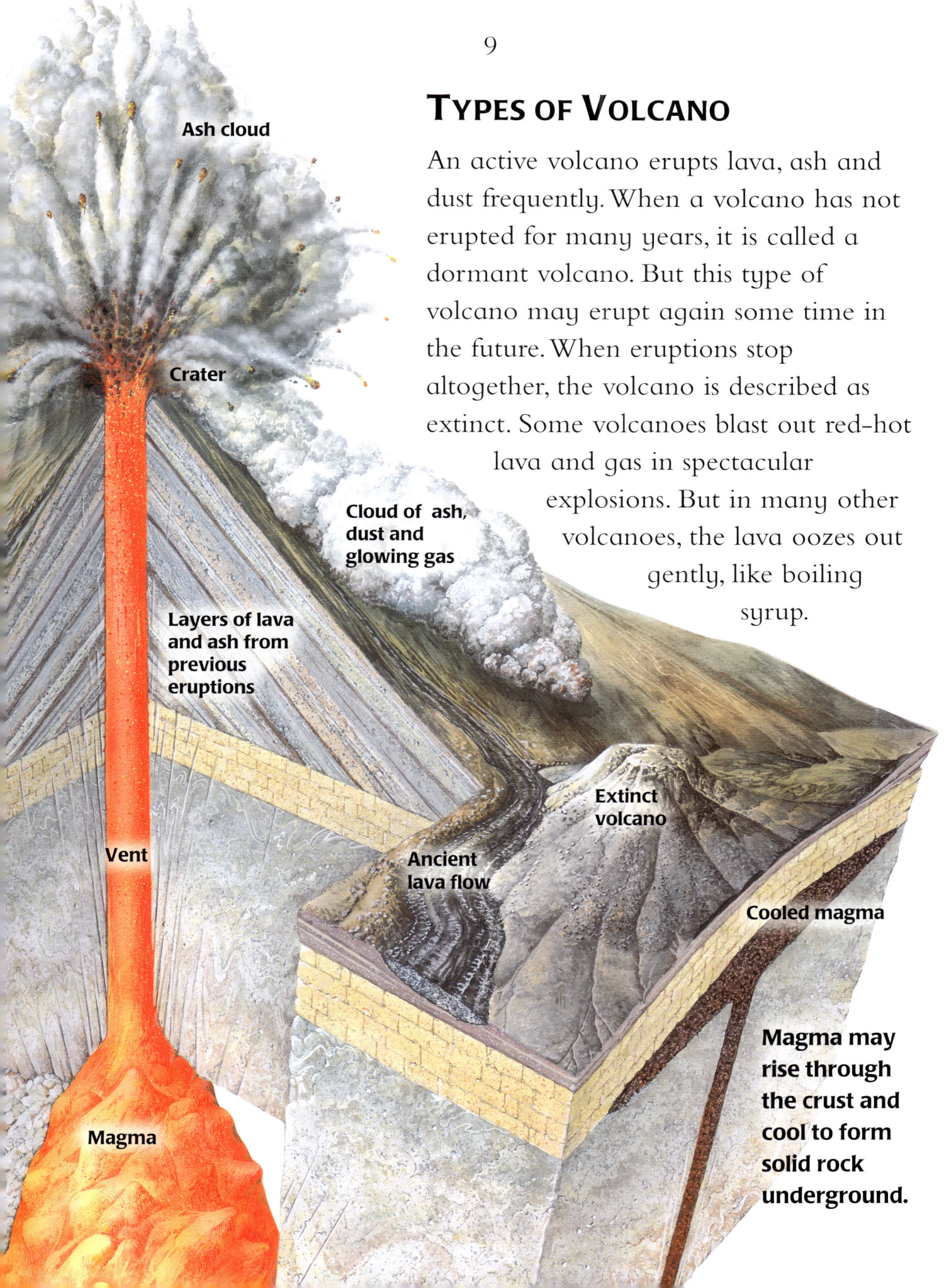

Magma may rise through the crust and cool to form solid rock underground.

EARTHQUAKES

AN EARTHQUAKE is the trembling or shaking of the ground. It is caused by the sudden movement of the rocks in the Earth's crust. This happens when the edge of one tectonic plate *(see page 6)* slides beneath or alongside another. The two plates may lock together for a while before the pressure becomes too much and the rocks snap apart.

EARTHQUAKE DAMAGE

It is mostly in towns and cities where earthquakes cause large loss of life. The sudden violent shaking of the ground may result in the collapse of buildings and bridges, pipes bursting and cables breaking. Fire or flooding also create great damage.

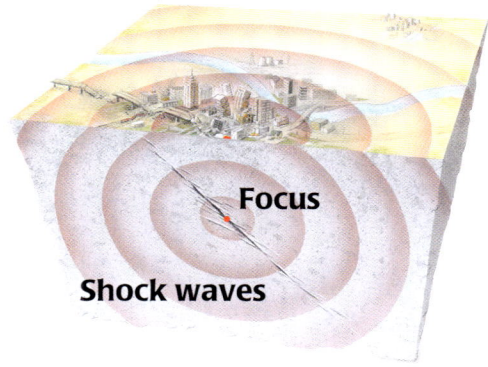

Focus
Shock waves

SHOCK WAVES

The place where the rocks snap is called the focus. Shock waves travel out in all directions. In a small earthquake, the ground will tremble only slightly. In a large one, it may shake violently for several minutes.

TSUNAMI!

A tsunami is caused by an earthquake on the sea bed. The sudden slip creates a series of fast-moving waves. When they reach coastal waters, they build up to immense heights.

HOW ROCKS ARE MADE

ROCKS are the hard materials that make up the Earth's crust. They lie both beneath the soil and the depths of the ocean. You can see them in cliffs along the seashore. Rocks are, themselves, made up from a solid mixture of minerals.

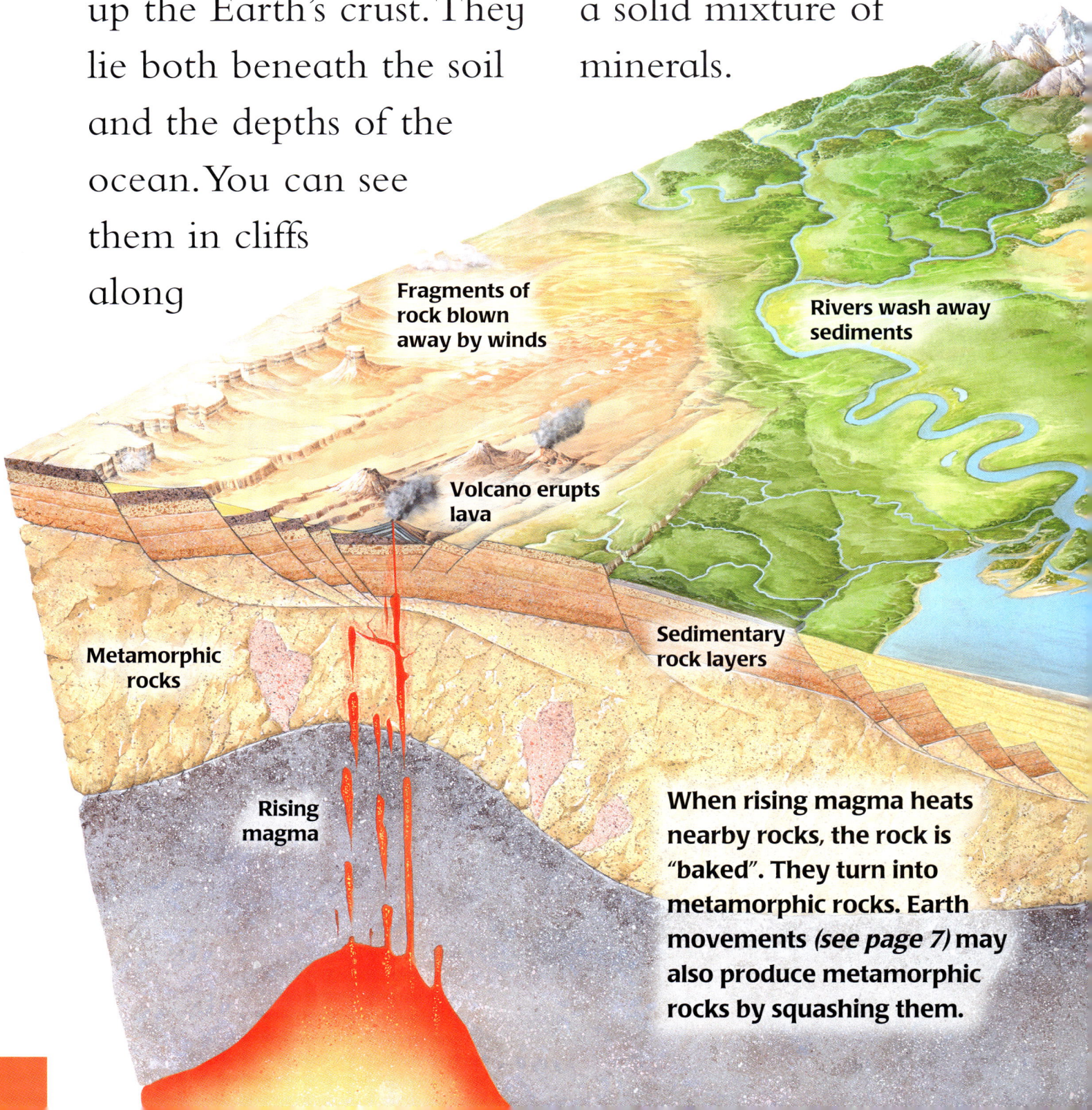

Fragments of rock blown away by winds

Rivers wash away sediments

Volcano erupts lava

Metamorphic rocks

Sedimentary rock layers

Rising magma

When rising magma heats nearby rocks, the rock is "baked". They turn into metamorphic rocks. Earth movements *(see page 7)* may also produce metamorphic rocks by squashing them.

This diagram shows part of the Earth's crust. Wind, rivers and glaciers wear down all kinds of rocks into fragments called sediments. These are washed away into lakes and seas.

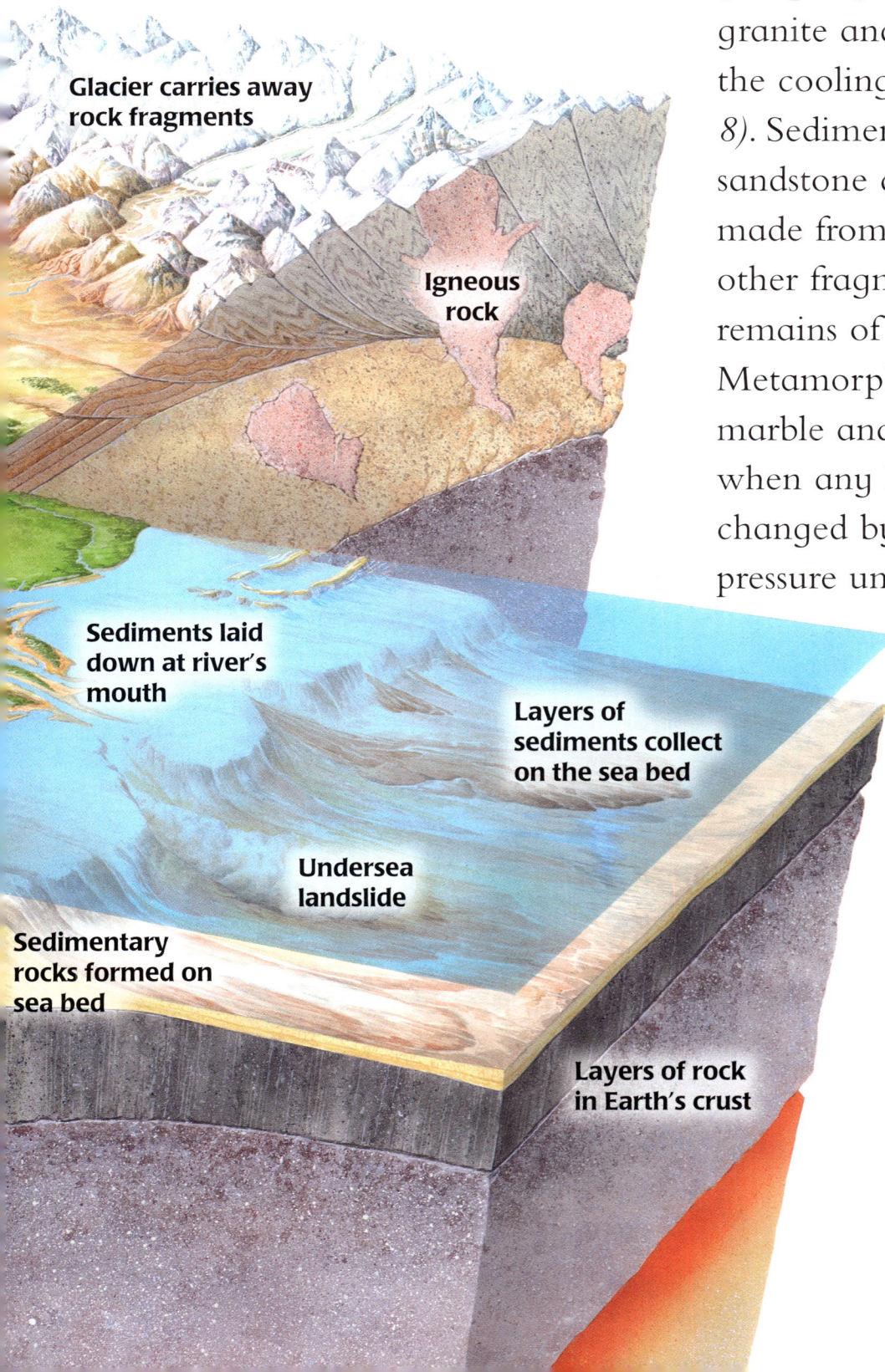

Glacier carries away rock fragments

Igneous rock

Sediments laid down at river's mouth

Layers of sediments collect on the sea bed

Undersea landslide

Sedimentary rocks formed on sea bed

Layers of rock in Earth's crust

TYPES OF ROCK

There are many kinds of rocks. They can be divided into three groups. Igneous rocks, such as granite and basalt, result from the cooling of magma (see page 8). Sedimentary rocks, such as sandstone and limestone, are made from sand, mud and other fragments of rock, or the remains of living things. Metamorphic rocks, such as marble and slate, are formed when any kind of rock is changed by great heat or pressure under the ground.

Many sediments are washed out to sea. As more layers settle on top of each other, the weight presses the fragments together. Eventually, they form rocks. Over millions of years, Earth move-ments may bring the sedimentary rock layers to the surface.

RIVERS

RIVERS are natural water channels. They carry rain or melted snow and ice downhill to lowlands, lakes and seas.

The force of running water wears away the rocks. This is called erosion.

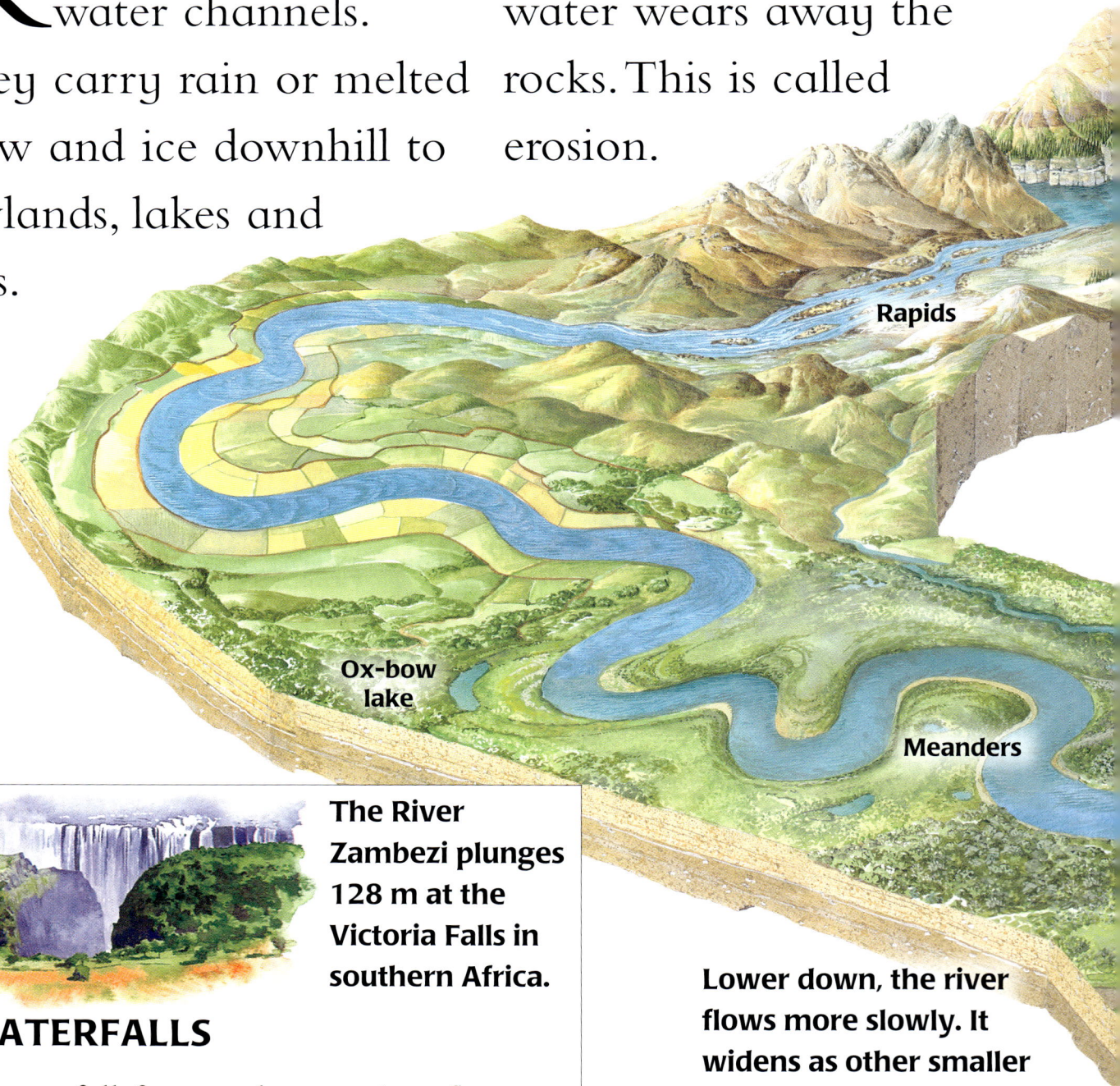

Rapids

Ox-bow lake

Meanders

The River Zambezi plunges 128 m at the Victoria Falls in southern Africa.

WATERFALLS

A waterfall forms where a river flows over a cliff, or where the rocks in its bed become easier to wear away. The water cascades over a "lip" of hard rock.

Lower down, the river flows more slowly. It widens as other smaller rivers, called tributaries, join it. Over flatter ground, the river flows in huge curves called meanders.

Glacier
meltwater

Mountain
lake

Waterfall

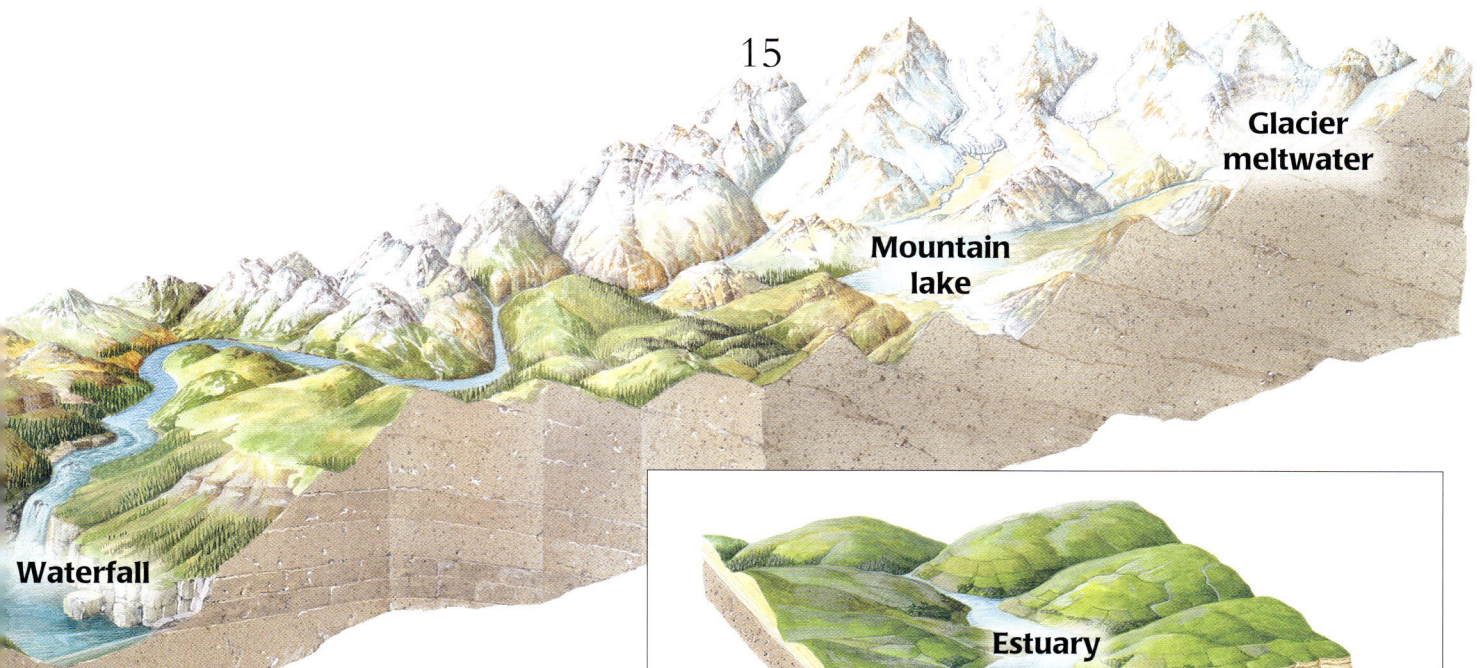

A river starts as a spring, rainwater collecting on sodden ground or meltwater from a glacier. Near its source, the river, often called a brook or stream, flows quickly. Its waters wash away soil and mud so that the stream bed is bare rock.

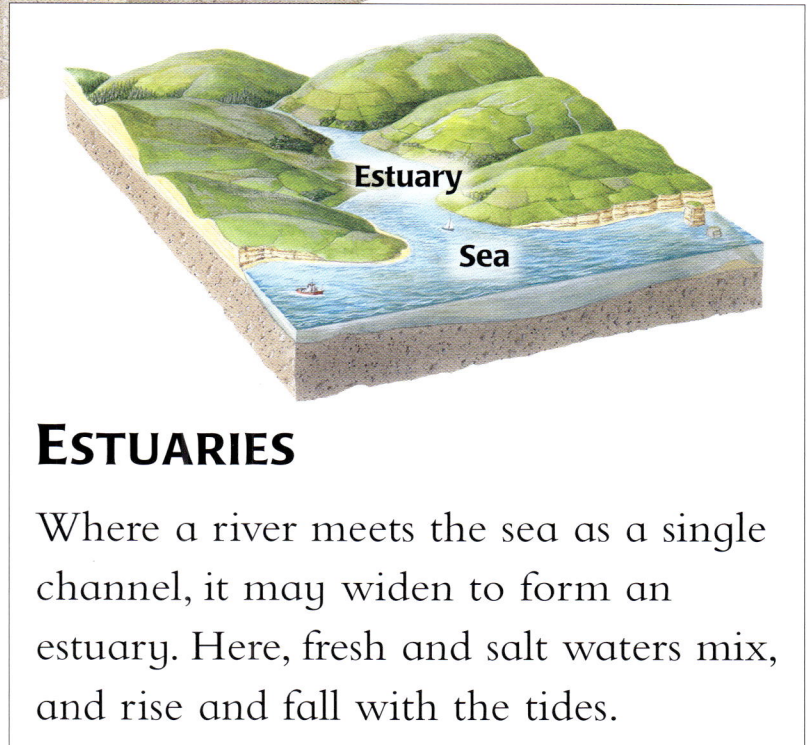

Estuary

Sea

ESTUARIES

Where a river meets the sea as a single channel, it may widen to form an estuary. Here, fresh and salt waters mix, and rise and fall with the tides.

The river finally enters the sea at its mouth. It may divide into many channels, forming a delta.

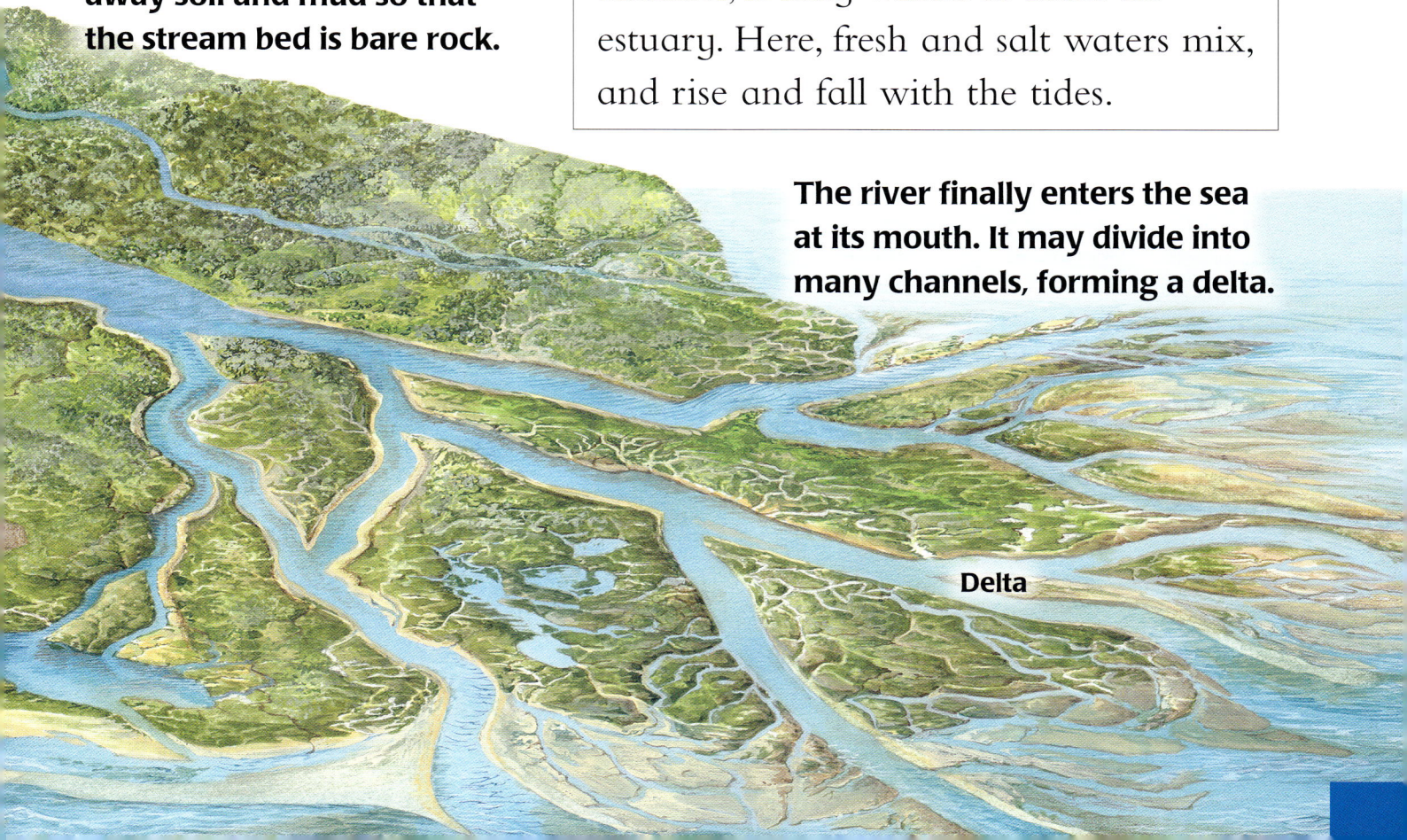

Delta

CAVES

CAVES are formed when water, flowing below ground, hollows out the rocks. You may also come across caves at the seashore, where waves crash against the cliffs. Limestone caves are often made up of a series of chambers, linked by tunnels and shafts. Some have lakes.

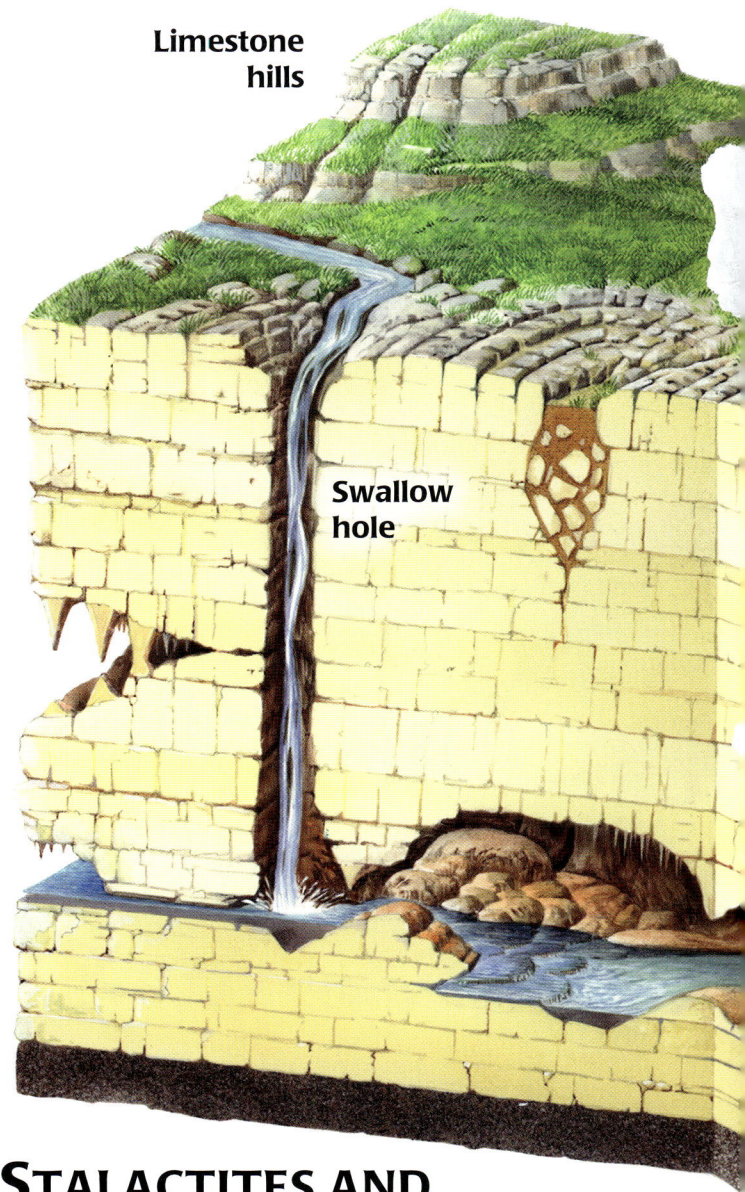

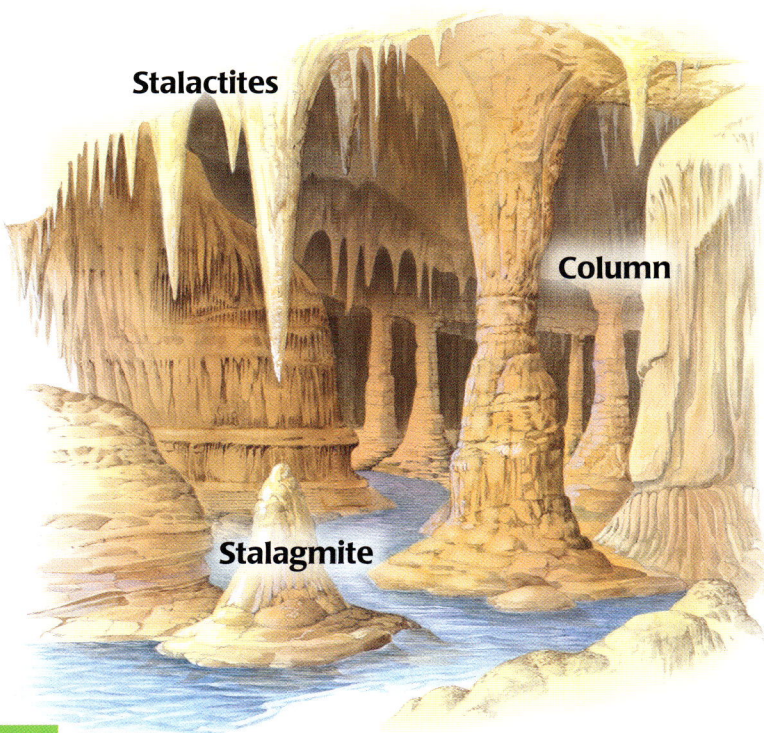

Limestone hills

Swallow hole

Stalactites

Column

Stalagmite

STALACTITES AND STALAGMITES

As water drips from the ceiling of a cave, the limestone dissolved in it hardens very gradually to form icicle-like stalactites. Stalagmites grow up from the floor where the drips fall. Sometimes they join the stalactites to form columns of rock.

This is a cross-section through an area of limestone rock.

LIMESTONE CAVES

Limestone may look like solid rock, but it contains millions of cracks. Rainwater seeps into these cracks. Over many years, the water dissolves the rock, widening the cracks and eventually forming caves.

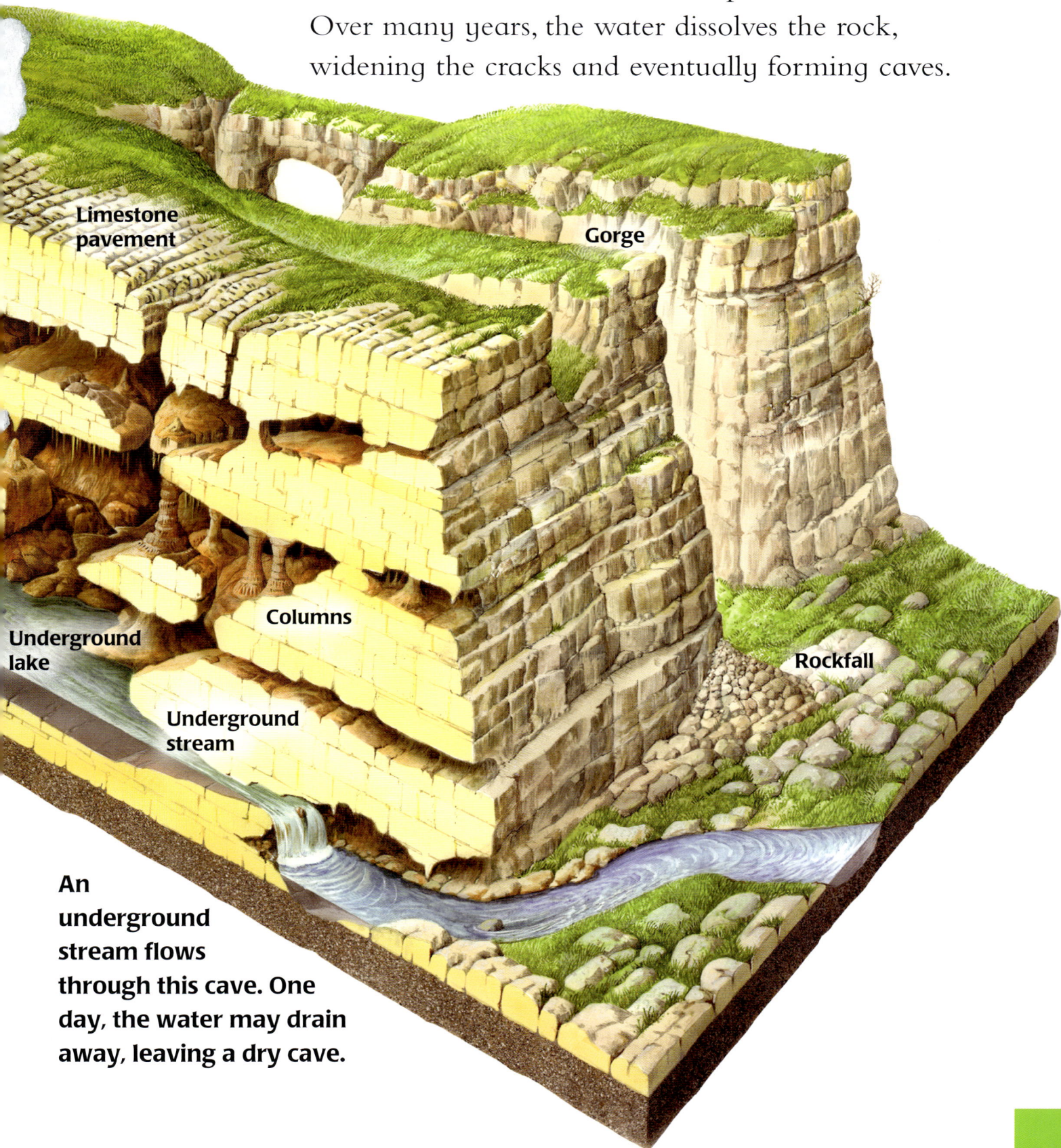

Limestone pavement

Gorge

Columns

Underground lake

Rockfall

Underground stream

An underground stream flows through this cave. One day, the water may drain away, leaving a dry cave.

GLACIERS

A GLACIER is a mass of ice that moves slowly downhill. It is made from layers of snow.

As the layers build up, the snow turns to ice. The ice becomes so thick and heavy, it starts to move.

Cirque (hollow where glaciers begin)

Moraines from two glaciers meet

End moraine

Meltwater streams

RIVERS OF ICE

As a glacier grinds its way down a valley, it gouges out loose rocks and carries them downhill. These rocks collect together in bands called moraines. Where two glaciers meet, their moraines merge together. Further down the valley where the glacier melts (at its snout), all the rocks are dumped in heaps known as end moraines. Where a glacier runs over steeper slopes, cracks, known as crevasses, form on its surface.

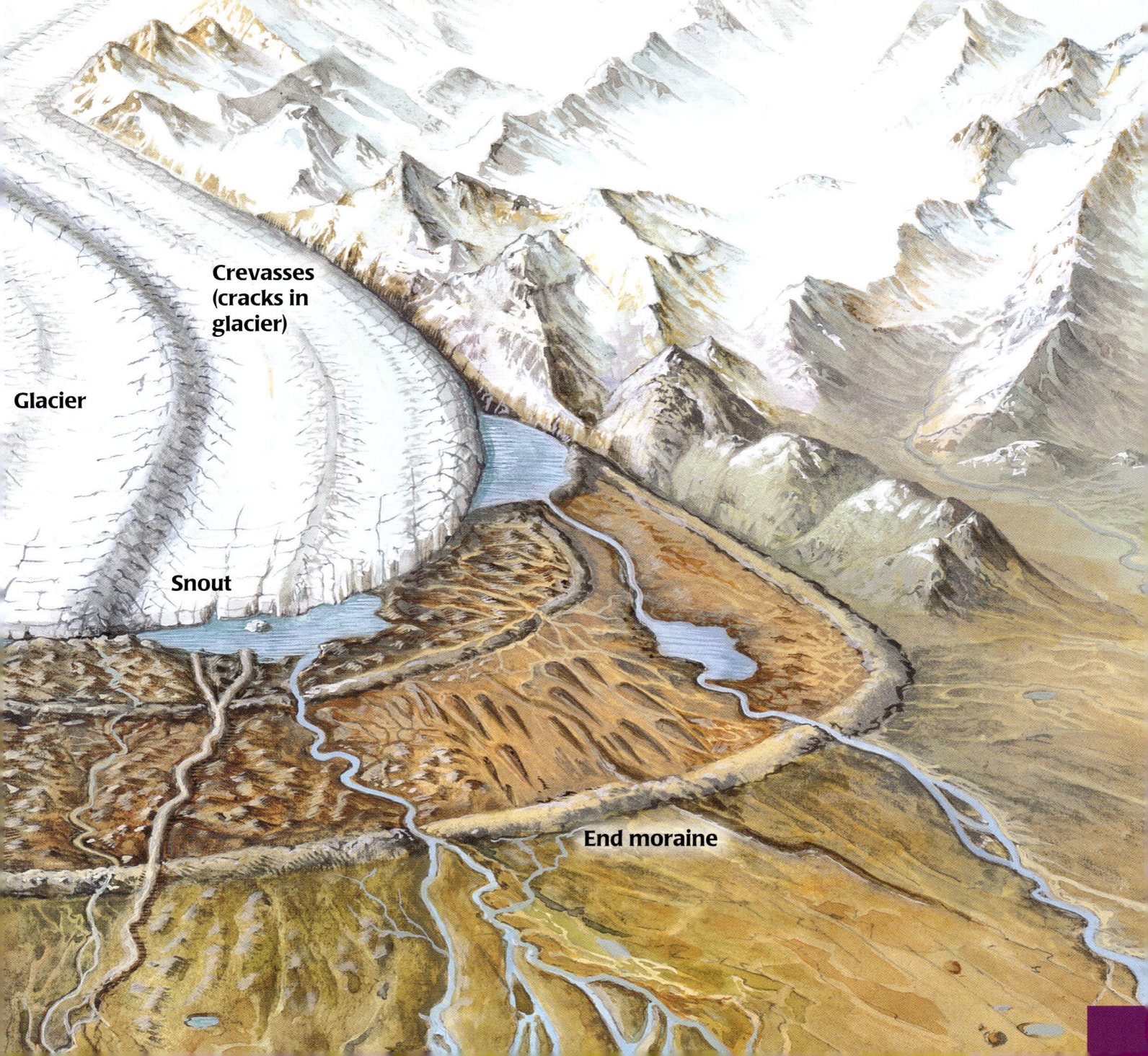

Crevasses (cracks in glacier)

Glacier

Snout

End moraine

DESERTS

Some desert mountain ranges have flat tops. They are called mesas.

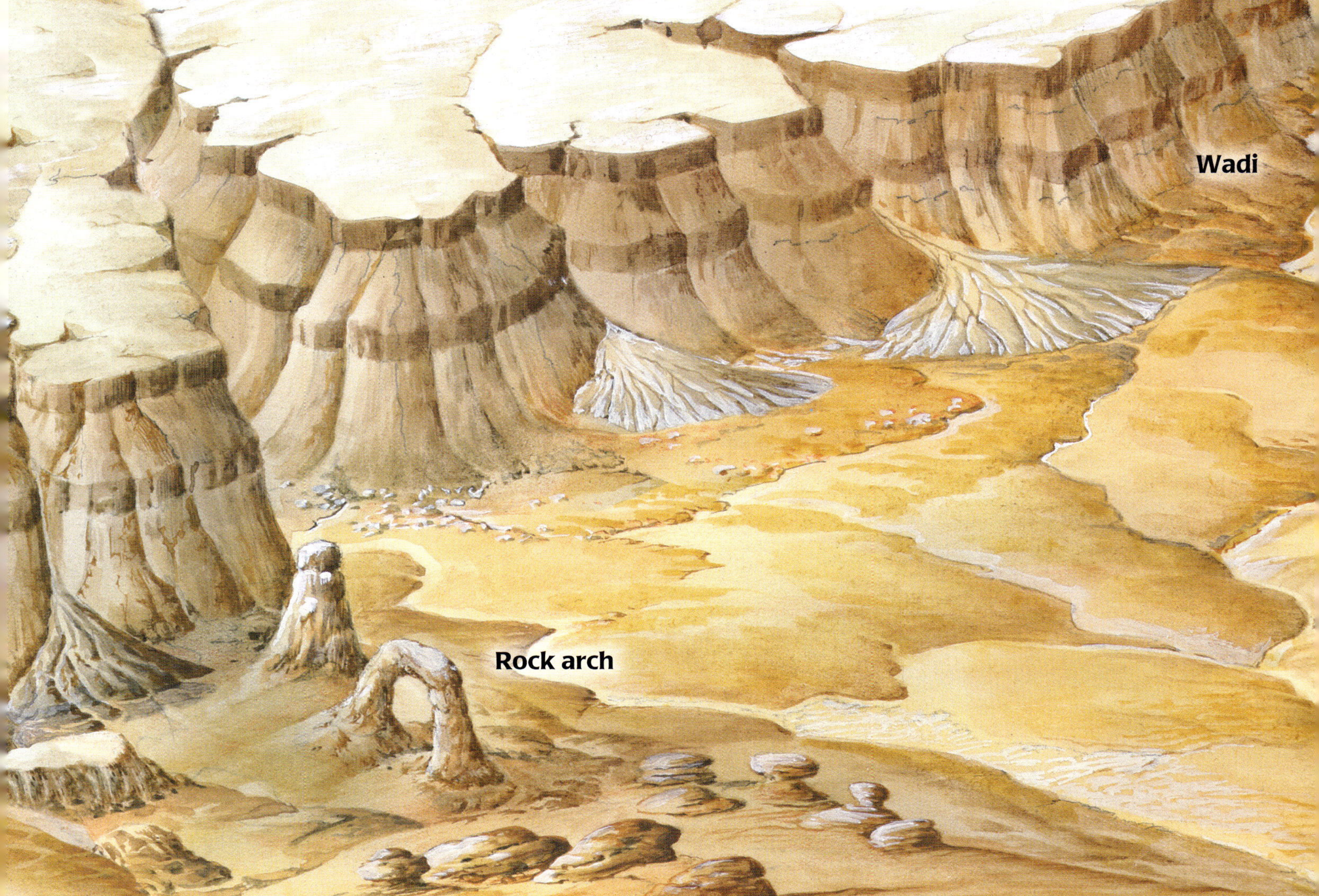

Wadi

Rock arch

DESERTS are found in areas where very little rain falls. Other than at oases, fertile spots in a desert, there is little sign of life. Many people think of deserts as vast areas of sand. In fact, only about a fifth of the world's hot deserts are sandy. Most are just bare rock and gravel. Antarctica is also a desert: very little snow ever falls there.

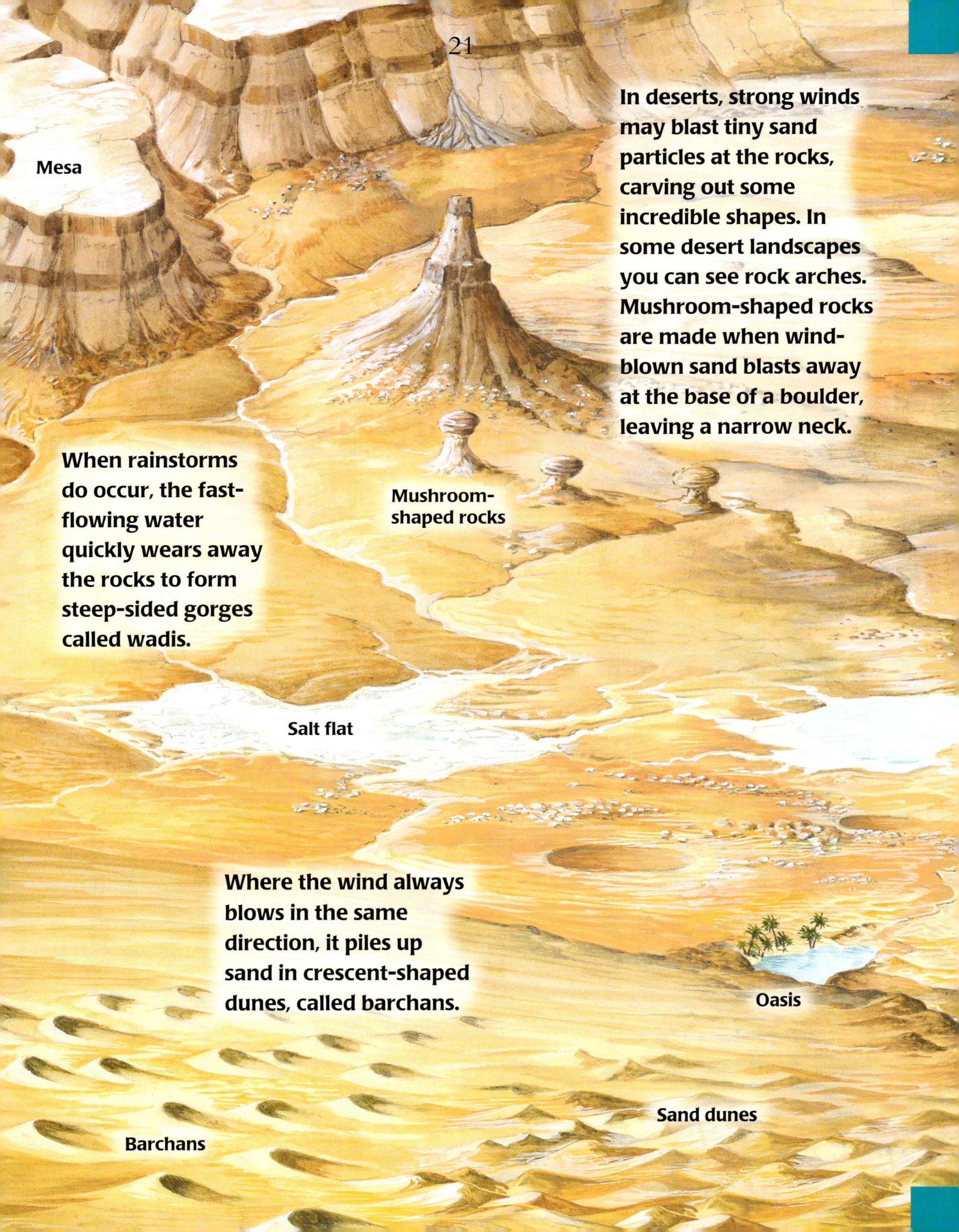

Mesa

In deserts, strong winds may blast tiny sand particles at the rocks, carving out some incredible shapes. In some desert landscapes you can see rock arches. Mushroom-shaped rocks are made when wind-blown sand blasts away at the base of a boulder, leaving a narrow neck.

When rainstorms do occur, the fast-flowing water quickly wears away the rocks to form steep-sided gorges called wadis.

Mushroom-shaped rocks

Salt flat

Where the wind always blows in the same direction, it piles up sand in crescent-shaped dunes, called barchans.

Oasis

Sand dunes

Barchans

WATER

THE OCEANS hold about 97% of the world's water. Some water is carried in the air as clouds. It may fall to the ground as rain or snow. Then it flows back to the ocean in rivers. This happens over and over again, all over the world. It is called the water cycle.

Water vapour in the air is carried by winds

Clouds form

Evaporation from oceans

Rain falls over oceans

EVAPORATION AND CONDENSATION

When water from oceans, rivers or lakes is heated by the Sun, it evaporates: it turns into an invisible gas called water vapour. This rises into the air and is blown by winds. As the air rises, it cools and starts to condense (turns back into a liquid) around tiny dust particles in the air. Millions of water droplets gather together to form clouds.

Ice or water droplets fall as snow or rain

Clouds form

Water evaporates from rivers, lakes or vegetation

Rivers carry water across land's surface

Water may seep down into the rocks. This groundwater will eventually flow down into the oceans.

Much of the water evaporated from the oceans falls directly back into the oceans as rain.

THE WATER CYCLE

Water evaporated from the oceans may be carried as water vapour across land. As it rises above high ground, it condenses and falls to earth as snow or rain. Rivers carry the water on the land's surface back to the ocean and the cycle begins again.

WEATHER AND CLOUDS

WEATHER is a word to describe the what is happening in the air: rain or snow, hot or cold, windy or still. The Sun's heat is vital to our weather. Some regions are warmer than others. Warm air rises, so cooler air flows in to replace it, producing winds. When air moves, it carries water vapour from one area to another *(see page 22-23)*.

Clouds form at different heights above the ground and have different shapes. They may be wispy, fluffy or flat.

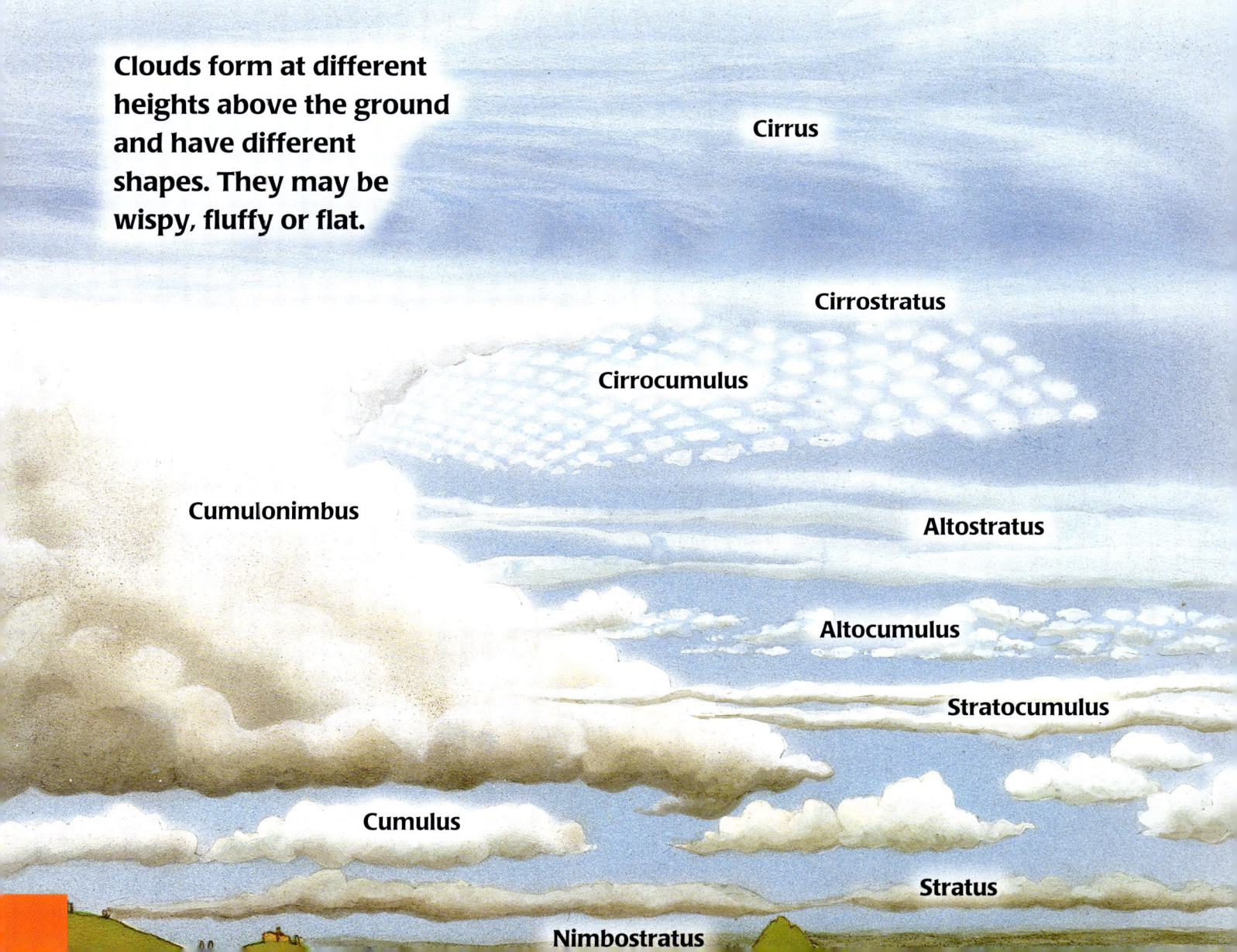

Cirrus

Cirrostratus

Cirrocumulus

Cumulonimbus

Altostratus

Altocumulus

Stratocumulus

Cumulus

Stratus

Nimbostratus

CLOUDS IN CLOSE-UP

Clouds consist of millions of tiny water droplets or ice particles. When water vapour in the air condenses, water droplets form around dust particles *(see page 22)*. If the temperature falls below freezing, the droplets turn to ice. They float in the air until they become too heavy. They then fall as rain or snow.

A FOGGY DAY

Fog or mist (a thin fog) is cloud that hugs the ground. It is often foggy when moist air cools at night, causing water droplets to form. Fog also forms when moist air is forced to rise over a hill.

At night, the ground cools quickly. Water vapour near the ground condenses, forming dew. This soaks everything – including spiders' webs.

If the temperature falls below freezing, the condensed water vapour turns into a layer of sparkling ice crystals, which we call frost.

STORMS

STORMY weather means high winds and heavy rain or snow. In some parts of the world, the extremely fast-moving winds of hurricanes and tornadoes may be powerful enough to cause severe damage and even loss of life. Heavy rainfall or blizzards may also result in floods, mudslides or avalanches in mountainous areas.

LIGHTNING

Thunderclouds form when warm, moist air rises quickly. As water droplets and ice crystals bump together, they produce electricity. We see this as lightning. The heat of the flash causes the air around it to expand rapidly, making the boom of thunder.

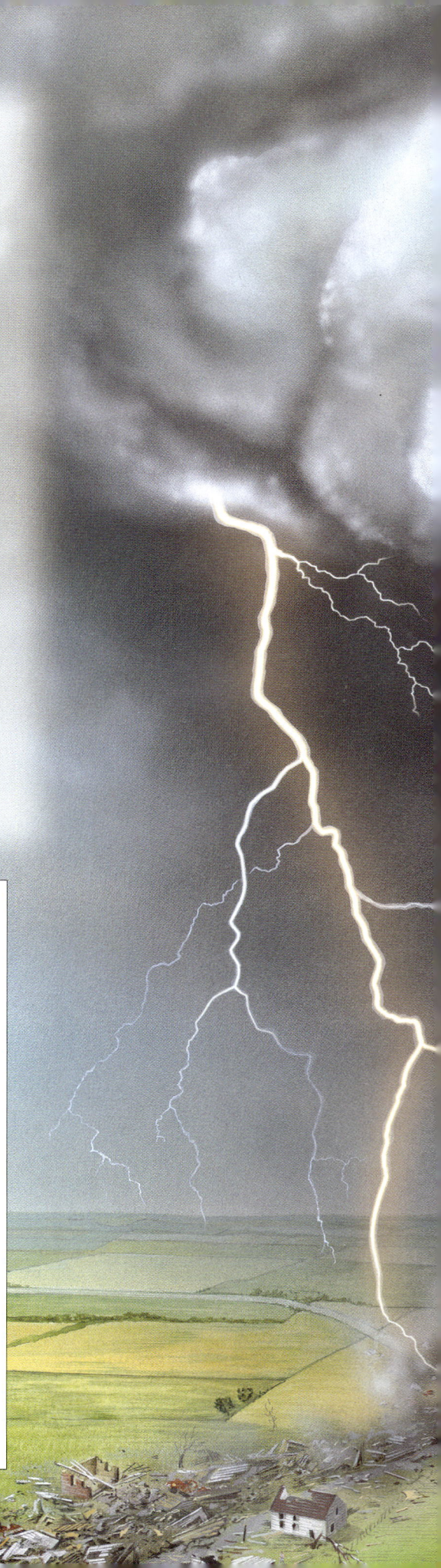

HURRICANES

A hurricane is a storm that occurs in tropical regions. It begins when warm, moist air rises high above the oceans. The air begins to swirl around in a spiral. Clouds form and massive downpours follow. Very powerful winds rage around a calm centre, called the "eye" of the storm. When a hurricane moves across land, it can cause great damage, including ripping up trees and overturning cars.

A tornado is a twisting column of air, swirling at up to 400 km per hour. Its base may be only 100 m across, but the winds are so powerful they destroy nearly everything in their path.

SEASONS AND CLIMATES

IN MANY parts of the world, the weather changes according to the time of year. These are the changing seasons. Different patterns of weather, including rainfall, winds and temperature, are found in different parts of the world. These patterns are called climates.

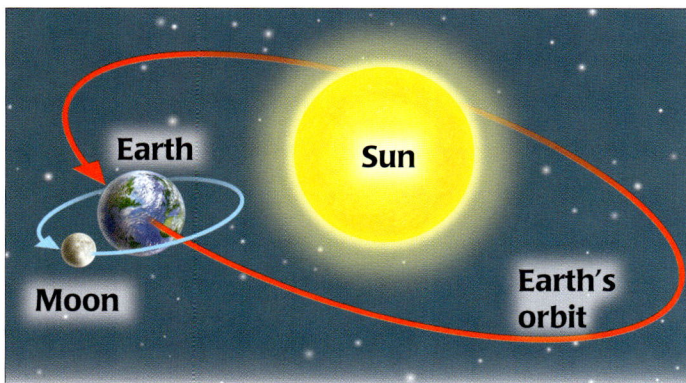

EARTH'S CLIMATES

Hot climates are found near the Equator where the Sun is closest. Polar regions, where the Sun is furthest away, are the coldest. In between are temperate lands which have warm summers and cool winters.

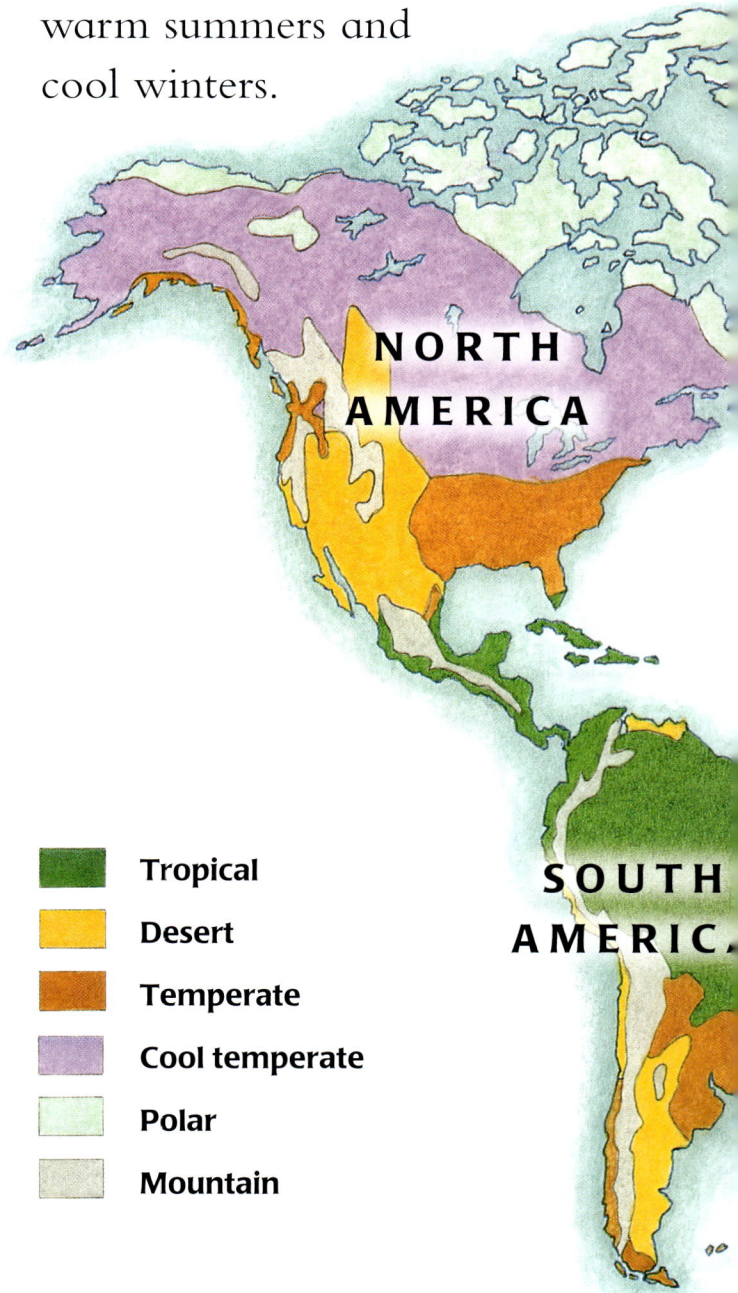

THE EARTH IN ORBIT

The Earth orbits the Sun in just over 365 days. The Moon orbits the Earth in about 27 days. The Earth spins once every 24 hours.

Tropical

Desert

Temperate

Cool temperate

Polar

Mountain

NORTH AMERICA

SOUTH AMERICA

21st June

Sun's rays

Sun's rays

22nd December

THE SEASONS

As the Earth spins round, it is not upright but tilted. When the northern half (the northern hemisphere) leans towards the Sun, the Sun is nearer. It is summer. Later in the year, the southern hemisphere is nearer the Sun and has its summer. The northern hemisphere is further away and has winter.

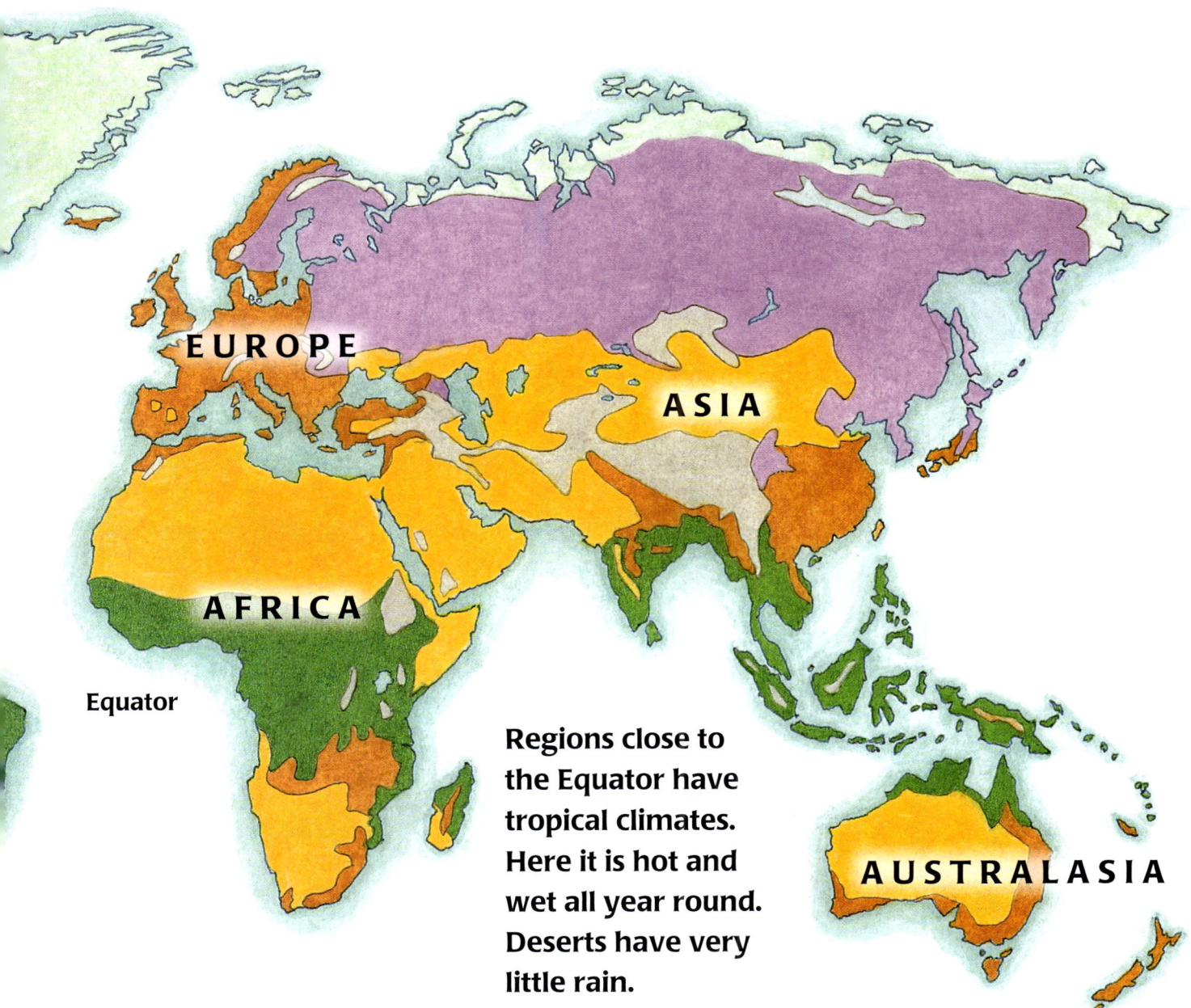

EUROPE

ASIA

AFRICA

Equator

AUSTRALASIA

Regions close to the Equator have tropical climates. Here it is hot and wet all year round. Deserts have very little rain.

GLOBAL WARMING

THE EARTH is getting warmer. Average temperatures worldwide have risen during the last century and there is no sign of this rise slowing. There is now a high risk that the ice caps will start to melt, raising sea levels every-where and changing world climates.

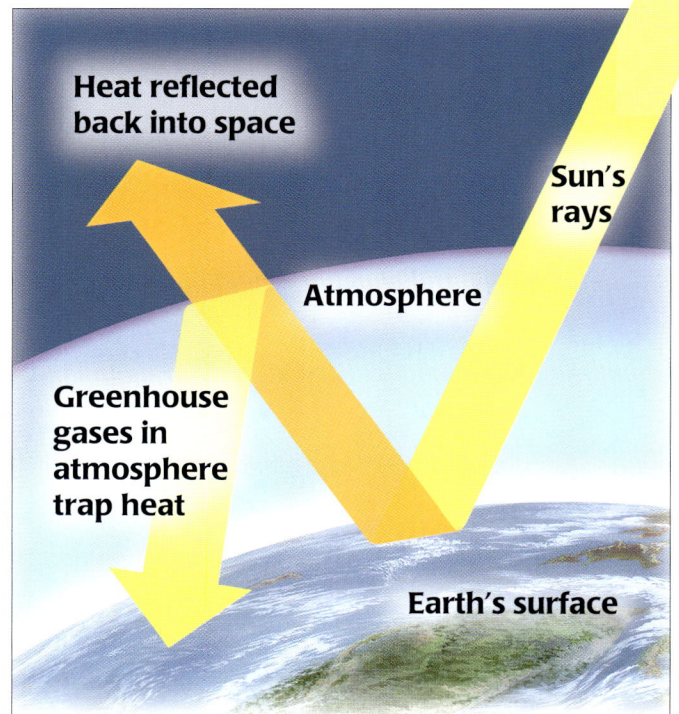

Heat reflected back into space

Sun's rays

Atmosphere

Greenhouse gases in atmosphere trap heat

Earth's surface

GREENHOUSE EFFECT

The atmosphere contains gases that stop all the Sun's heat escaping. These gases act like the glass in a greenhouse. They help keep the Earth's surface warm.

WHY IS IT HAPPENING?

Global warming is probably caused by the greenhouse effect *(see panel)*. Human activities have resulted in a large increase of greenhouse gases, such as carbon dioxide, in the atmosphere. Vehicles and power stations give off exhaust gases from burning oil or coal ("fossil fuels"). These add billions of tonnes of carbon dioxide to the atmosphere. Plants will usually absorb (take in) carbon dioxide as part of their natural life cycle. But the destruction of forests around the world means there are fewer plants to absorb the gas.

If melted ice cause sea levels to rise, it may result in many coastal cities being flooded by sea water. To avoid this catastrophe, people must reduce the amount of greenhouse gases in the air by burning fewer fossil fuels.

INDEX

TITLES IN THIS SERIES